Fluorine

and the Halogens

Nigel Saunders

www.heinemann.co.uk/library

Visit our website to find out more information about Heinemann Library books.

To order:
☎ Phone 44 (0) 1865 888066
▤ Send a fax to 44 (0) 1865 314091
▢ Visit the Heinemann Bookshop at www.heinemann.co.uk/library to browse our catalogue and order online.

First published in Great Britain by Heinemann Library, Halley Court, Jordan Hill, Oxford OX2 8EJ, part of Harcourt Education.
Heinemann is a registered trademark of Harcourt Education Ltd.

Produced for Heinemann by Discovery Books Ltd

Editorial: Dr Carol Usher and Sarah Eason
Design: Ian Winton
Illustrations: Stefan Chabluk
Picture Research: Vashti Gwynn
Production: Edward Moore

Originated by Ambassador Litho Ltd
Printed and bound in Hong Kong, China by South China Printing Company

ISBN 0 431 16997 7
07 06 05 04
10 9 8 7 6 5 4 3 2 1

British Library Cataloguing in Publication Data
Saunders, N. (Nigel)
   Fluorine and the halogens.
   - (The periodic table)
   546.7'3

A full catalogue record for this book is available from the British Library.

Acknowledgements
The publishers would like to thank the following for permission to reproduce photographs:
Corbis pp**8** (José Luis Pelaez), **9** (Gordon Ray Gainer), **10** (David Samuel Robbins), **12**, **19** (Lester V Bergman), **21** (John Heseltine), **22** (Dave Bartruff), **24** (Steve Jay Crise), **27** (Tom Stewart), **28**, **30**, **39** (Bettmann), **29** (Paul A Souders), **32** (Tom & Dee McCarthy), **37** (Paul Steel), **40** (Jim Sugar), **43** (Hanan Isachar), **44** (Bill Varie), **54**; Discovery Picture Library pp**4**, **47**; Science Photo Library pp**14** (Martin Dohrn), **16** (Krafft, Explorer), **17** (Charles D Winters), **23** (US Department Of Energy), **25** (Dr P Marazzi), **31** (John Mead), **34** (Juergen Berger, Max-Planck Institute), **41** (Gaillard, Jerrican), **46** (Cordelia Molloy), **48** (Simon Fraser), **49** (Claude Nuridsany & Marie Perennou), **50** (Martyn F Chillmaid), **51** (BSIP, Chassenet), **52** (John Paul Kay, Peter Arnold Inc.), **53** (A McClenaghan), **55** (Oulette & Theroux, Publiphoto Diffusion), **56** (American Institute of Physics).

Cover photograph of fluoride toothpaste, reproduced with permission of Corbis.

The author would like to thank Angela, Kathryn, David and Jean for all their help and support.

Contents

Words appearing in bold, **like this**, are explained in the Glossary

Elements and atomic structure

Everything around you is made from chemicals, including the air you breathe, the water you drink, the food you eat and you too! There are millions of different chemicals. Most of them are solids, but some are gases, such as air, and others are liquids, such as water. However, no matter how simple or complex they are, all chemicals have one thing in common: they are made from just a few simple substances called **elements**.

All the things you can see here, including the people, water slide and the boat, are made from some of the millions of substances in the world. Most of these substances, including the water, are compounds.

Elements and compounds

Chemicals that cannot be broken down into simpler substances using chemical **reactions** are called elements. Around ninety elements occur naturally and scientists have learned how to make over twenty more using **nuclear reactions**. Over three-quarters of the elements are metals, such as iron and sodium, and the rest are non-metals, such as oxygen and chlorine. Elements can join together in chemical reactions to make **compounds**. Iron and oxygen, for example, react together to make iron oxide and the reaction between sodium and chlorine creates sodium chloride. Most of the chemicals in the world are compounds, made up of two or more elements chemically joined together.

Atoms

Every chemical, whether it is an element or a compound, is made up of tiny particles called **atoms**. Each element contains just one type of atom and compounds are made from two or more types of atom joined together. Although we can see most of the chemicals around us, individual atoms are too tiny to be visible, even with a light microscope. Out of the five halogens astatine has the largest atoms, but even if you could make yourself ten million million times smaller than you are now, you would still be taller than an astatine atom!

Subatomic particles

Atoms are made from even smaller objects called **subatomic particles**. At the centre of each atom there is a **nucleus**, which contains **protons** and **neutrons**. **Electrons** are subatomic particles that are even smaller than protons and neutrons. They are arranged around the nucleus in different layers, or 'shells', in an arrangement resembling that of the planets around the Sun. In fact most of an atom is empty space!

proton

neutron

electron

nucleus

This is a model of an atom of fluorine. Each fluorine atom contains nine protons and ten neutrons, with nine electrons arranged in two shells or energy levels around the nucleus.

Groups

Elements all react in different ways, which makes chemistry both exciting and mystifying. Once chemists had discovered a lot of elements, they tried to order them to make things clearer. Dimitri Mendeleev, a Russian chemist, was the most successful at doing this. He devised a table in 1869 where each element was put into one of eight **groups**. All the elements in a group were similar to each other and this made it much easier for chemists to predict what would happen in their experiments. Mendeleev's table was so successful that the modern **periodic table** is based on it.

The periodic table, fluorine and the halogens

Chemists have built upon Mendeleev's table and the modern **periodic table** is the result. Each vertical column in the periodic table is called a **group** and all the **elements** in a group have similar chemical properties. There are eighteen groups altogether. The horizontal rows are called **periods**. The number of **protons** in the **nucleus** of each **atom** (the **atomic number**) gets bigger as you go from left to right across a period.

The manner in which an element **reacts** is determined by the number of **electrons** its atoms have and the way the electrons are arranged in their shells. Each element in a group has the same number of electrons in the shell furthest from the nucleus, called the outer shell. The elements in group 1, for example, are reactive metals with one electron in their outer shell. The halogens, on the other hand are reactive non-metals with seven electrons in their outer shells. The periodic table gets its name because there is a regular or periodic recurrence of these different chemical properties.

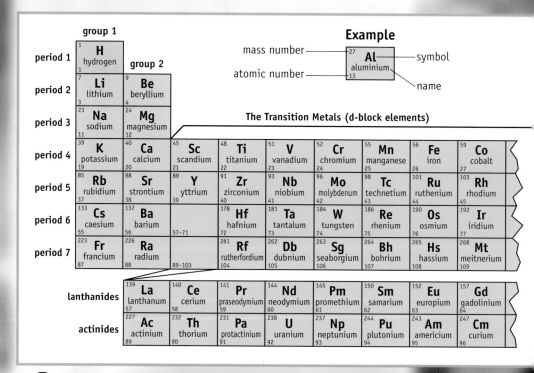

The properties of the elements change gradually as you go down a group. In group 1 the elements become more reactive. When they are added to water, lithium, at the top of the group, fizzes; potassium, from the middle, bursts into flames; while caesium, from near the bottom of group 1, explodes violently! The halogens also have gradual changes as you go down their group, as you will see.

Fluorine and the halogens

The elements in group 7 are often called the halogens because they react with metals to produce salts – the word halogen comes from the Greek meaning salt-former. The halogens and the many **compounds** they form are very useful to us. In this book, you are going to find out all about fluorine, the other halogens and how they are used.

▼ *This is the periodic table of the elements. Group 7 contains fluorine, chlorine, bromine, iodine and astatine, which are all non-metals.*

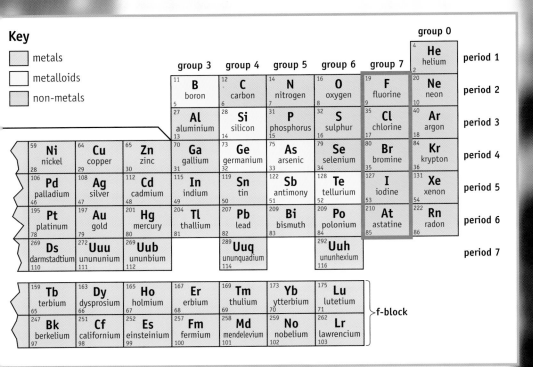

Key
- metals
- metalloids
- non-metals

group 0

	group 3	group 4	group 5	group 6	group 7		
						4 **He** helium 2	period 1
	11 **B** boron 5	12 **C** carbon 6	14 **N** nitrogen 7	16 **O** oxygen 8	19 **F** fluorine 9	20 **Ne** neon 10	period 2
	27 **Al** aluminium 13	28 **Si** silicon 14	31 **P** phosphorus 15	32 **S** sulphur 16	35 **Cl** chlorine 17	40 **Ar** argon 18	period 3

59 **Ni** nickel 28	64 **Cu** copper 29	65 **Zn** zinc 30	70 **Ga** gallium 31	73 **Ge** germanium 32	75 **As** arsenic 33	79 **Se** selenium 34	80 **Br** bromine 35	84 **Kr** krypton 36	period 4
106 **Pd** palladium 46	108 **Ag** silver 47	112 **Cd** cadmium 48	115 **In** indium 49	119 **Sn** tin 50	122 **Sb** antimony 51	128 **Te** tellurium 52	127 **I** iodine 53	131 **Xe** xenon 54	period 5
195 **Pt** platinum 78	197 **Au** gold 79	201 **Hg** mercury 80	204 **Tl** thallium 81	207 **Pb** lead 82	209 **Bi** bismuth 83	209 **Po** polonium 84	210 **At** astatine 85	222 **Rn** radon 86	period 6
269 **Ds** darmstadtium 110	272 **Uuu** unununium 111	269 **Uub** ununbium 112		289 **Uuq** ununquadium 114		292 **Uuh** ununhexium 116			period 7

| 159 **Tb** terbium 65 | 163 **Dy** dysprosium 66 | 165 **Ho** holmium 67 | 167 **Er** erbium 68 | 169 **Tm** thulium 69 | 173 **Yb** ytterbium 70 | 175 **Lu** lutetium 71 | f-block |
| 247 **Bk** berkelium 97 | 251 **Cf** californium 98 | 252 **Es** einsteinium 99 | 257 **Fm** fermium 100 | 258 **Md** mendelevium 101 | 259 **No** nobelium 102 | 262 **Lr** lawrencium 103 | |

Elements of group 7

There are five **elements** in **group** 7, fluorine, chlorine, bromine, iodine and astatine. Fluorine and chlorine are gases at room temperature, bromine, in the middle of group 7, is a liquid, whereas iodine and astatine are solids. Bromine is the only liquid non-metal element. Mercury is the only liquid metal element.

19	**F**	**fluorine**
	fluorine	symbol: F • atomic number: 9 • non-metal
9		

What does it look like?   Fluorine is a pale yellow gas that is slightly **denser** than air. It is the most **reactive** of all the elements, reacting with almost everything else! This makes it very dangerous and difficult to store.

Where is it found?   Fluorine is far too reactive to be found naturally as a free element. Instead, it is found in various **compounds** within **minerals** such as cryolite and fluorspar.

What are its main uses?   You will not come across fluorine in your everyday life because it is so dangerous, but it is used industrially to purify uranium for nuclear power stations. Fluorine compounds are added to toothpaste and drinking water to help prevent tooth decay and the non-stick surface on many pans is a plastic that contains fluorine. Other fluorine compounds are used in the manufacture of light bulbs and computer chips.

Fluorine compounds, such as sodium fluoride and sodium monofluorophosphate, are added to toothpastes to protect our teeth from tooth decay.

35	Cl	chlorine
	chlorine	
17		

chlorine

symbol: Cl • atomic number: 17 • non-metal

What does it look like?   Chlorine is a dense, green-yellow gas. You will recognize chlorine's sharp smell if you have ever been to a swimming pool. Chlorine is not as reactive as fluorine, but it will react with most other elements. It is also poisonous and was used as a chemical weapon in World War I.

Where is it found?   Chlorine is only found naturally in compounds as it is very reactive. Sodium chloride is the most common chlorine compound and is found in halite or rock salt. The oceans contain vast quantities of sodium chloride and chlorine is the main non-metal in seawater. Sylvite and carnallite are other minerals that contain chlorine.

What are its main uses?   Chlorine and its compounds are widely used to kill harmful bacteria in swimming pools and drinking water. Chlorine compounds are also the active ingredients of most disinfectants and bleaches. It is used in the manufacture of antiseptics and plastics such as polyvinylchloride (PVC). Chlorine compounds are needed to make a vast range of everyday items, including fabrics, paper, dyes and medicines. A range of compounds called chlorofluorocarbons (CFCs) contain chlorine and fluorine. CFCs were used widely in aerosol cans, fridges and fast food containers, but are now being replaced by other substances because they damage the Earth's ozone layer.

Chlorine or chlorine compounds, such as ▶ sodium hypochlorite, are added to drinking water to kill harmful bacteria.

More elements of group 7

80
Br
bromine
35

bromine

symbol: Br • atomic number: 35 • non-metal

What does it look like? Bromine is a **reactive**, red-brown liquid. It easily vaporizes to produce a poisonous red vapour with a sharp smell, similar to that of chlorine. This makes bromine difficult and dangerous to handle.

Where is it found? Like fluorine and chlorine, bromine is too reactive to occur naturally as a pure **element**. Bromine is found in various **compounds** in the Earth's crust and in seawater. It is particularly concentrated in the Dead Sea, a land-locked salt lake between Jordan and Israel in the Middle East.

What are its main uses? The biggest single use of bromine is in the manufacture of fire-retardant chemicals, which are substances that make plastics and other materials resistant to fire. It is also used in photographic chemicals, medicines, water-purifying chemicals and pesticides (chemicals that farmers and gardeners use to kill pests).

▼ *Silver bromide and silver iodide are important ingredients in photographic film.*

127
I
iodine
53

iodine

symbol: I • atomic number: 53 • non-metal

What does it look like?   Iodine crystals are shiny and so dark that they look almost black. At room temperature they easily turn into a dark purple vapour, which has a sharp smell similar to the smell of chlorine. Iodine is poisonous and reactive, just like the other halogens, and it must be handled carefully. It dissolves slightly in water to produce a brown solution.

Where is it found?   Iodine is only found naturally in compounds. These are rare in the Earth's crust, but they are concentrated in some salt deposits. Seawater contains a small proportion of iodine compounds, although there are high concentrations in seaweed.

What are its main uses?   Iodine is an important trace **mineral** in our diet. Without it we suffer from a disease called goitre. Iodine compounds are added to table salt to avoid iodine deficiency. Iodine is used in the manufacture of photographic chemicals, ink and medicines.

210
At
astatine
85

astatine

symbol: At • atomic number: 85 • non-metal

What does it look like?   Astatine is a shiny black solid with some properties of metals. It is difficult to study because it is extremely rare, but it is less reactive than iodine and it appears to react with metals in a similar way to the other halogens.

Where is it found?   Astatine is formed from uranium by natural **nuclear reactions** and there are only a few grams of it in the whole of the Earth's crust at any one time. Scientists can make it in tiny amounts using artificial nuclear reactions.

What are its main uses?   Astatine has no uses apart from scientific research.

Trends in group 7

Mendeleev grouped the halogens together because they are similar to each other in many ways. Although they are all reactive non-metals, and exist as molecules made from two atoms joined together, they are not identical to each other. Many of their physical properties change gradually going down the **group**, such as their state and colour. A gradual change is called a trend.

Not just one atom, but two

*Halogen atoms are joined by chemical **bonds** to form molecules. Halogen molecules are called diatomic because 'di' is from the Greek for twice and each one contains two atoms joined together. The chemical formula for fluorine gas is F_2 and it is Cl_2 for chlorine gas. Similarly, bromine is Br_2 and iodine is I_2.*

What a state!

The state of a substance refers to whether it is a solid, liquid or gas. The state of the halogens at room temperature changes as you go down group 7. This is because the melting and boiling points of the halogens gradually increase as you go down the group.

Room temperature is above the melting and boiling points of fluorine and chlorine, so both **elements** are gases. On the other hand, the melting and boiling points of iodine and astatine are above room temperature, so these elements are solids. Bromine is interesting because its melting point is below room temperature, while its boiling point is above, which is why it is normally a liquid at room temperature.

Bromine is a red-brown liquid at room temperature. It easily vaporizes, forming a red vapour with a sharp smell that is similar to that of chlorine. ▶

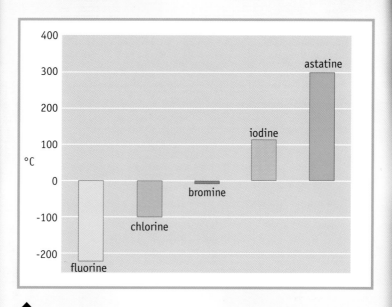

▲
This bar chart shows the melting points of the halogens. The melting points increase as you go down the group.

Bigger molecules mean higher boiling points

Halogen molecules have weak chemical bonds between them. When the halogens are heated strongly enough, these bonds break, separating the molecules and letting them escape as a gas. If these bonds are strong, you need a lot of energy to break them and the boiling point is high. The molecules become bigger as you go down group 7. Big molecules have stronger bonds between them than small molecules. This means that more energy is needed to break the bonds, giving a high boiling point.

Coloured vapours

The halogens are either coloured gases at room temperature or produce coloured vapours when they are heated. Although chemists in movies often seem to be surrounded by coloured liquids and gases, most gases are actually colourless – just think about the air you breathe. Going down group 7, the vapours become darker. At the top of the group, fluorine is a pale yellow gas, followed by chlorine, which is green-yellow. Bromine with its red vapour comes next, followed by iodine with its purple vapour.

The salt formers

All the halogens **react** with metals to produce salts, just as sodium and chlorine react together to make sodium chloride, which is common table salt.

The word equation for the reaction between sodium and chlorine is:

sodium + chlorine → sodium chloride

Sodium chloride is common table salt, used to flavour boiled eggs and other food. 'Iodized' table salt also contains iodine compounds such as potassium iodide, which protects us against illnesses caused by too little iodine in our diet.

Getting less reactive

The halogens become less reactive as you go down **group** 7. Fluorine is the most reactive **element** of all. When fluorine touches sodium (a very reactive metal from group 1), the sodium burns violently to produce white sodium fluoride. However, sodium must be heated first before chlorine reacts with it, then it burns quickly to produce white sodium chloride.

The halogens react with iron, especially if it is made from very fine strands called iron wool. When chlorine gas is passed over hot iron wool, the iron glows brightly and immediately clouds of brown iron chloride are produced. Contrastingly, when bromine vapour is passed over hot iron wool it glows and slowly produces some brown iron bromide. There is only a very slow reaction when iodine vapour is passed over hot iron wool. This produces some brown iron iodide – most of the purple iodine vapour just escapes without reacting.

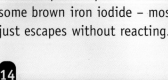

The word equation for the reaction of iron with bromine is:

iron + bromine → iron bromide

Astatine, at the bottom of the group, is the least reactive halogen, but it is difficult to study because it is **radioactive** and very rare.

Gain an electron

An **atom** will be reactive if its outer shell is not completely filled with **electrons**. All halogen atoms have seven electrons in their outer shells and need to gain one more to have a completely full outer shell with eight electrons. This happens when a halogen atom reacts with a metal atom. The smaller the halogen atoms are, the easier it is for them to acquire electrons. Fluorine atoms are the smallest in the group and it is very simple for them to gain an electron, so fluorine is very reactive. The atoms get bigger as you go down group 7. It is very difficult for astatine atoms to gain electrons because they are the largest in the group, so astatine is the least reactive halogen.

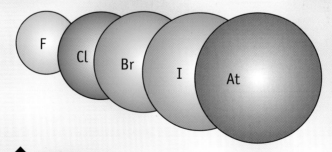

▲
The halogen atoms get bigger as you go down group 7.
Fluorine atoms are only half the diameter of astatine atoms.

Becoming an ion

When a halogen atom fills its outer shell by gaining an electron it becomes a halide **ion**. Fluorine atoms become fluoride ions and chlorine atoms become chloride ions.

Don't go near the water!

When the halogens are added to water, they don't just dissolve in it, they **react** with it to produce acids. There is a trend in how they react with water, similar to their trend with metals.

Chlorine water and more

Fluorine reacts violently with water to produce oxygen gas and a very corrosive acid called hydrofluoric acid. The reaction also produces ozone, which is a type of oxygen. Ozone has a sharp, electrical smell and causes stinging eyes and breathing difficulties.

When volcanoes erupt, they release molten rock and various gases into the air. Water vapour, carbon dioxide and sulphur dioxide are the most common gases, but volcanoes also release chlorine and fluorine. The fluorine reacts with water, forming poisonous hydrofluoric acid, which damages the lungs, skin and eyes of people and animals that, unfortunately, happen to be near by.

Chlorine dissolves easily in water to produce a pale yellow solution usually called chlorine water. However, some of the chlorine reacts with the water to produce a mixture of hydrochloric and hypochlorous acids. These acids are not as dangerous as hydrofluoric acid, but are still corrosive. When water is treated with chlorine to kill harmful bacteria, just enough is added so that the bacteria are killed without making it harmful to us.

Bromine water, a clear orange solution, is formed when bromine dissolves in water. Some of the bromine reacts with the water to produce hydrobromic and hypobromous acids. Iodine dissolves in water with difficulty to make a brown solution called iodine water. This is made easier by adding potassium iodide. Iodine water is acidic because it contains a little hydriodic acid and hypoiodous acid. If you spill iodine water, the iodine stains your skin brown and your cotton shirt purple.

Displacement reactions

Chlorine is more reactive than iodine, so it replaces iodine in iodine **compounds**. You can see this happening if chlorine water is added to colourless potassium iodide solution because the mixture turns brown when iodine forms. Potassium chloride is made as well. This is called a **displacement reaction** and it is sometimes said that chlorine acts as a 'chemical bully' because it pushes iodine out of its compounds.

◄ *In this experiment, chlorine gas is being bubbled into potassium bromide solution, causing a reaction that produces yellow-brown bromine gas.*

The word equation for the reaction between chlorine water and potassium iodide is:

chlorine + potassium iodide → potassium chloride + iodine

Likewise chlorine displaces bromine from colourless potassium bromide solution, so it turns orange-brown. Bromine, in turn, displaces iodine from colourless potassium iodide solution so it becomes brown. These reactions are used industrially to produce bromine and iodine.

The word equations for the reactions between chlorine water and potassium bromide, bromine water and potassium iodide are:

chlorine + potassium bromide → potassium chloride + bromine

bromine + potassium iodide → potassium bromide + iodine

Testing for halogens and photography

Chemists use silver nitrate solution to test their chemicals to see if they contain any dissolved halogen **compounds**.

Testing for halogens

When silver nitrate solution is added to sodium chloride solution the two chemicals **react** to produce sodium nitrate and silver chloride. The sodium nitrate dissolves, so you cannot see it, but the silver chloride is insoluble and forms tiny white particles. This is called a **precipitate** and makes the mixture look cloudy white.

The word equation for testing a liquid for dissolved sodium chloride (common salt), using silver nitrate solution is:

silver nitrate + sodium chloride $\rightarrow$ sodium nitrate + silver chloride

Silver nitrate solution can also be used to test for bromides and iodides. When it is added to sodium bromide a cream-coloured precipitate of silver bromide forms. If silver nitrate solution is added to sodium iodide a yellow precipitate of silver iodide appears.

The word equations for using silver nitrate solution to find out if a liquid contains dissolved sodium bromide or sodium iodide are:

silver nitrate + sodium bromide $\rightarrow$ sodium nitrate + silver bromide

silver nitrate + sodium iodide $\rightarrow$ sodium nitrate + silver iodide

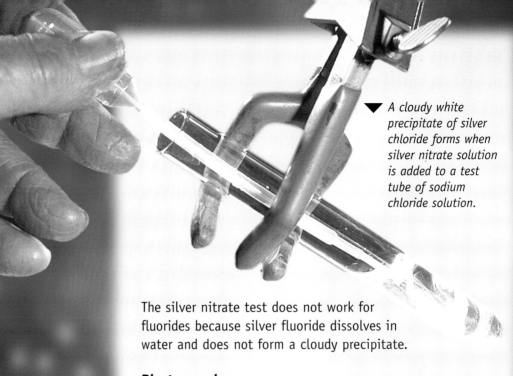

A cloudy white precipitate of silver chloride forms when silver nitrate solution is added to a test tube of sodium chloride solution.

The silver nitrate test does not work for fluorides because silver fluoride dissolves in water and does not form a cloudy precipitate.

Photography

Silver chloride, silver bromide and silver iodide gradually turn black if they are left in the light, although this does not happen to silver fluoride. The light causes the silver halides to decompose or break down to form tiny particles of silver that appear black. These reactions are used to form the picture in photographic film and photographic paper.

William Fox Talbot, an English scientist, patented a form of photography called 'Talbotype' in 1841. He coated paper with silver chloride solution and dried it in the dark to make photographic paper. Photographs were taken by laying an object on the paper and leaving it in sunlight. The paper stayed white where it was covered up, but where it was exposed to light the silver chloride turned black.

Modern film contains silver bromide and silver iodide trapped in thin layers of a substance called gelatine. There is just one layer in black and white film, but colour film has three layers that also contain dyes sensitive to different colours of light. Digital photography uses light-sensitive electronic devices to make a photograph, rather than light-sensitive halogen compounds. The demand for silver halides will decrease as digital photography becomes more popular.

Fluorine

Fluorine is a poisonous, pale yellow gas. It is the most **reactive element** in the **periodic table** and although it does not react with air it reacts vigorously with other non-metals and metals. Powdered silicon, sulphur and aluminium, for example, all explode with a white flash in fluorine. This extreme reactivity makes fluorine very difficult and dangerous to handle.

Towards a new element

Fluorine **compounds** have been used for several centuries, but for most of that time nobody realized that fluorine itself existed. A **mineral** called fluorspar (calcium fluoride, CaF_2) was first used in the sixteenth century by metal workers as a flux. Fluxes are substances that lower the melting point of metal **ores**, making it easier to **extract** the metals from them. In fact, fluorine is named after the Latin word 'fluere', which means to flow.

In the eighteenth century it was discovered that fluorspar and sulphuric acid reacted together to make a very powerful acid, which we now know is hydrofluoric acid (HF). Glassmakers found this useful for etching patterns into their glass. Carl Scheele, the Swedish chemist who discovered chlorine, managed to make some pure samples of hydrofluoric acid in 1771. He believed that fluorspar and the glass-etching acid both contained a new element. Scheele and other chemists set out, on what proved to be a dangerous mission, to isolate it.

Dying to discover fluorine

Chemists could not isolate fluorine from its **compounds** using chemical reactions because it is far too reactive. When Alessandro Volta, an Italian scientist, invented the electric battery in 1880, chemists passed electricity through lots of different chemicals to see what would happen. Those who tried hydrofluoric acid were in for a nasty shock. Hydrofluoric acid breaks down into hydrogen and fluorine when electricity is passed through it. Immediately these two gases meet they explode and several chemists were killed, injured or poisoned by the results of their experiments. Fluorine was eventually produced in 1886 by a French chemist called Henri Moisson. He was awarded the Nobel prize in 1906 for his efforts.

Getting at fluorine

Fluorine compounds are found in minerals such as fluorspar and cryolite (sodium aluminium fluoride, Na_3AlF_6). Over four million tonnes of fluorspar are mined in the world each year and more than half of this comes from the USA. Moisson's original method is used to extract fluorine, but on a much larger scale. Electricity is passed through a molten mixture of potassium fluoride and hydrogen fluoride. Fluorine is produced at the positive electrode, piped off and stored under pressure in stainless steel gas cylinders.

◀ *Deposits of the mineral fluorspar (calcium fluoride) in the Blue John Cavern in Derbyshire, England.*

Hydrofluoric acid

Fluorine is used to make a huge range of fluorine **compounds**, but the gas itself has no direct uses because it is so **reactive**. It can be stored in stainless steel cylinders, but they must be really clean because the fluorine will react vigorously with any oil or grease. Fluorine even reacts with most of the **elements** from **group** 0, often called the noble gases, which are extremely unreactive. If xenon and fluorine are heated to 300 °C, they react together to produce xenon difluoride, which is a white solid.

Etching glass

Hydrofluoric acid is a strong acid made by reacting fluorspar and sulphuric acid together. It is very difficult to store and handle safely and it produces fumes that are easily absorbed through the skin, causing severe burns. Hydrofluoric acid is used to make etched glass. This is glass with white, slightly rough areas wherever the acid has attacked it. Patterns are etched in decorative glass panels for showers and windows. Pearl effect light bulbs with frosted glass provide a much softer light than light bulbs with clear glass. Glass may also be etched by sandblasting, as hydrofluoric acid is dangerous.

These fine patterns have been etched into this glass using hydrofluoric acid. ▶

The word equation for producing hydrofluoric acid from fluorspar (calcium fluoride) is:

calcium fluoride + sulphuric acid → calcium sulphate + hydrofluoric acid

Nuclear fluorine

Uranium is a **radioactive** metal used to make atomic bombs and fuel for nuclear power stations. Natural uranium has several **isotopes**, but is mostly uranium-238 with only about 0.7 per cent uranium-235. The '238' or '235' part of the name is the **mass number**. However, nuclear fuel and atomic bombs must contain a much greater proportion of uranium-235 than this. This means that the uranium-235 must be separated from the uranium-238 to produce 'enriched uranium'. To do this the uranium has to be converted into a gas called uranium hexafluoride (UF_6).

The word equation for producing uranium hexafluoride is:

uranium oxide + hydrofluoric acid $\rightarrow$ uranium hexafluoride + water

This reaction actually happens in several stages.

Uranium hexafluoride gas containing uranium-235 **atoms** weighs slightly less than if it has uranium-238 atoms, which means it can be separated in a centrifuge. This is a machine that spins the gas at very high speeds. The heavier gas is flung to the edges of the centrifuge, leaving the uranium hexafluoride containing uranium-235 near the centre. When uranium hexafluoride is heated with a reactive metal such as magnesium, uranium is produced.

◀ *This is the inside of a gas centrifuge, which is used to produce 'enriched' uranium for nuclear power stations by spinning uranium hexafluoride gas at high speed.*

Isotopes
*Isotopes are atoms of an element that have the same number of **protons** and **electrons**, but different numbers of **neutrons**. Different isotopes of an element behave identically in chemical reactions.*

Look after your teeth!

Bacteria live on the surface of the teeth in plaque, producing acid from the sugars in our food and drink. The acid **reacts** with the hard outer layer of our teeth, called enamel, dissolving some of the **minerals** in it. Saliva is slightly alkaline, so it eventually **neutralizes** the acid, but if we have too many sugary foods and drinks a hole or cavity may eventually form in the enamel. Bacteria can get into the dentine layer underneath, causing the cavity to get even bigger. Eventually the soft layer at the centre of the tooth, called the pulp, can be affected. This contains nerves, so tooth decay can be very painful. Regular brushing, flossing and a sensible diet help to avoid this.

This dentist is filling a tooth ▶
damaged by tooth decay. Fluorine
compounds in toothpastes and
drinking water help to protect teeth.

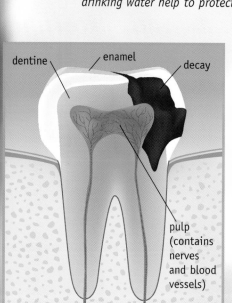

◀ *This diagram shows a section through a tooth damaged by tooth decay. It can take months or years for a cavity to develop in a tooth.*

Fluoride toothpaste

The fluorine **compounds** in toothpastes are sodium fluoride (NaF) or sodium monofluorophosphate (Na_2PO_3F), although they are just called fluorides. These compounds protect teeth from tooth decay in several ways. Calcium and other minerals naturally move in and out of the tooth enamel. If minerals are lost from the enamel because of acid attack, fluorides increase the movement of fresh minerals to the surface of the tooth, improving the repair process.

The quality of the enamel produced is also better. Fluorides help make enamel stronger in the growing teeth of young children, so that the enamel can resist acid attack. They also make it more difficult for bacteria to produce acids in the mouth.

Water fluoridation

If the concentration of fluorides is less than 0.3 mg in a litre of water they are unlikely to help fight tooth decay, so fluorides are deliberately added to drinking water in several countries. In the USA, fluoridated water is supplied to more than half the population; in the UK over ten per cent of the population receives it, mainly in the Midlands and north east of England.

What's in the water?

Fluorine compounds such as sodium hexafluorosilicate (Na_2SiF_6) and hexafluorosilicic acid (H_2SiF_6) are added to drinking water. The amount of fluoride in the water is usually 1 mg per litre.

Too much of a good thing

Water in some parts of the world, such as North Africa, India and China, naturally contains a lot of fluorides. Larger doses of fluorides can cause fluorosis, which affects teeth and bones. Brown areas may appear on the tooth enamel and joints can become stiff and painful. Many countries do not fluoridate their drinking water because of concerns about fluorosis.

Water suppliers that deliberately add fluorides to the water carefully control levels to reduce tooth decay without causing this problem.

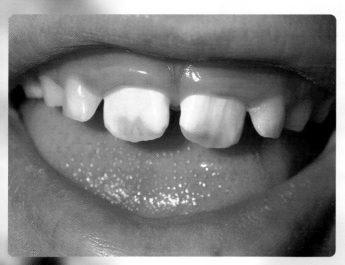

◀ *Fluorine compounds are useful for protecting teeth, but too many of them can cause fluorosis, which produces brown stains.*

Fluorine in plastics

Although fluorine is very **reactive**, its **compounds** are generally not.

Sulphur hexafluoride

Sulphur hexafluoride (SF_6) is an unreactive gas that is used when magnesium is being cast. Casting involves pouring molten magnesium into a mould, then letting it cool and solidify into shape. If this is done in air the magnesium will react readily with oxygen and nitrogen. To prevent this happening, the air around the liquid magnesium is replaced with unreactive sulphur hexafluoride.

Sulphur hexafluoride is useful in high-voltage transformers and switches, as it is a very good electrical insulator. When electricity is used at high voltages it can make very large sparks called arcs, rather like lightning. High-voltage equipment is usually sealed inside containers of sulphur hexafluoride gas at high pressure to stop arcs happening.

PTFE

Poly(tetrafluoroethene), or PTFE, is a plastic with some very useful properties. It was discovered accidentally by Roy Plunkett in 1938. He was investigating gases made from fluorine compounds and found that tetrafluoroethene **molecules** could join up end to end to make a white plastic. The chemical **bonds** in each molecule are very strong, so PTFE is very unreactive. As each molecule can easily slide over each other, PTFE is also very slippery. It is probably better known as Teflon, which is the trade name given to it by DuPont, Plunkett's employer. You may have used non-stick Teflon-coated pans, but the plastic has many other uses.

Modern tent fabrics may contain a special layer made with PTFE. It lets water vapour from perspiration out of the tent but prevents large droplets of rainwater getting in. ▶

Making PTFE

The chemical formula for tetrafluoroethene is C_2F_4. The two carbon atoms in the molecule are joined by two chemical bonds. When PTFE is being made, one of these bonds breaks in each tetrafluoroethene molecule. This allows thousands of tetrafluoroethene molecules to join on to each other, end to end, making PTFE.

When plumbers join pipes together they wrap PTFE tape around the metal thread in the joint to make a watertight seal. PTFE powder is added to lubricating oils and greases to make them more slippery, and to paints to give them a water-resistant finish when they are dry. The chemical industry lines tubes and other equipment with PTFE, which protects them from corrosive chemicals. Moving parts in machinery are often coated with PTFE and television cables contain a protective layer of it. Fibres containing PTFE are widely used in waterproof 'breathable' fabrics to make many things, like sportswear, sleeping bags and tents.

Chlorine

Chlorine is a poisonous green-yellow gas with an easily recognizable smell. It is less **reactive** than fluorine, but does react with most other **elements**, especially if they are heated. When burning sodium is lowered into a jar of chlorine gas there is a vigorous reaction. Sodium chloride is produced and so much heat that the sodium burns in the chlorine. Chlorine is **denser** than air and tends to fill cellars and hollows in the ground if it is released, making it particularly dangerous.

Poison gas

Chlorine is a poisonous gas that causes a tight chest, lung damage and suffocation. Death can happen in minutes if the air contains more than 0.1 per cent chlorine, although its smell would give you a warning at much lower concentrations. Chlorine was the first poison gas used to kill troops. During World War I, the German army killed thousands of Canadian and French troops when they released it in Belgium, in 1915. The use of poison gas in wars was banned by the Geneva Protocol, an international treaty signed in 1925.

▲
Chlorine gas was used to poison troops in World War I. In this pretend gas attack in 1918, American soldiers demonstrate what would happen to anyone who forgot their gas mask.

A new element – are you sure?

Carl Scheele discovered chlorine in 1774, while investigating a black **mineral**, called pyrolusite. He added this to hydrochloric acid or muriatic acid as it was called then, and a choking green-yellow gas was produced. Scheele realized that he had discovered a new metal, which turned out to be manganese. What he didn't know was that he had also discovered a new non-metal element. He thought the green-yellow gas was a **compound**.

The English chemist, Sir Humphry Davy, eventually realized that chlorine was an element in 1810. He produced chlorine gas by passing electricity through a solution of sodium chloride (common table salt). Davy named the gas after 'chloros', the Greek word for 'pale green'.

▲
The oceans are very salty. Each litre contains about 26 g of sodium chloride, the main salt in seawater.

The briny blue sea

The sea is salty because it contains dissolved sodium chloride and other salts, such as potassium chloride. Every litre of seawater contains 19 g of chlorine as chloride **ions**. The oceans are so vast that they contain twenty-five thousand trillion tonnes of chlorine, enough for us to continue **extracting** it for hundreds of millions of years.

Extracting chlorine

Chemists make small amounts of chlorine using potassium manganate(VII) and hydrochloric acid. Potassium manganate(VII), or potassium permanganate, consists of purple crystals. When hydrochloric acid is added to them, they immediately react with it to produce chlorine gas. Chlorine is produced on an industrial scale using a modified version of Davy's method and involves passing electricity through a concentrated solution of sodium chloride.

Sodium chloride

Sodium chloride, or common salt, is the most abundant chlorine **compound** and there are vast amounts of it in the sea and in underground salt deposits. More than two hundred million tonnes of salt are produced each year, not just to flavour food and treat icy roads in winter, but as an important raw material for the chemical industry.

Rock salt and sea salt

When the water in seawater evaporates, it leaves the dissolved salts behind. There are large underground deposits of rock salt in various places around the world, formed when water in ancient oceans evaporated. These include Cheshire in the UK, Michigan in the USA and Western Australia. Salt may also be left on the surface when the water in ancient oceans or salt lakes evaporates, producing salt flats. In many parts of the world, people deliberately make large, shallow lagoons on the coast. The Sun's heat evaporates the water, leaving deposits of sea salt behind that can be used by cooks to flavour food.

Flat out for a record

Salt flats, such as the Bonneville Salt Flats in Utah, are huge, level areas covered in salt. They are very popular with people trying to beat land speed records. These people drive specially designed cars, often powered by jet engines from aircraft. Salt flats provide the large expanse of flat land needed to make their record-breaking runs safely.

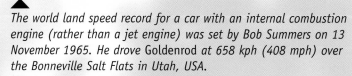

▲

The world land speed record for a car with an internal combustion engine (rather than a jet engine) was set by Bob Summers on 13 November 1965. He drove Goldenrod at 658 kph (408 mph) over the Bonneville Salt Flats in Utah, USA.

Winter roads

Roads and paths are de-iced in the winter using rock salt. The melting point of ice is normally 0 °C, but this is reduced when salt is added. This causes the ice to thaw, even when the temperature is below 0 °C. Although using salt is a cheap way to de-ice winter roads, salt makes steel rust faster, causing damage to vehicles and bridges. It can also harm roadside plants, so other salts, such as magnesium chloride, may be used instead in some areas.

◀ Iron and steel rust when they are in contact with air and water. However, the salt in seawater speeds up the rusting process considerably.

Chloride in our bodies

Although we need sodium chloride in our diet mainly for the sodium it contains, chloride **ions** are the most abundant negatively charged ions in our blood and are needed by our digestive system to make the hydrochloric acid contained in our stomachs. Stomach acid is very strong, with a pH value of about 1. This is nearly as strong as the acid you use in school chemistry lessons, which explains why your throat and mouth sting so much when you are sick. Hydrochloric acid helps to kill the harmful bacteria that we swallow with our food and provides the acid conditions needed for the digestive **enzymes** in the stomach to do their job properly.

Electrolysis of brine

Concentrated sodium chloride solution is called brine. When electricity is passed through brine, chlorine gas is produced at the positive electrode and hydrogen gas is produced at the negative electrode.

The chlor-alkali industry

The **electrolysis** of brine also produces a very useful alkali called sodium hydroxide, which is widely used in the manufacture of artificial fibres for clothing, paper, detergents and soap. The industry is usually called the chlor-alkali industry because the electrolysis of brine produces chlorine and an alkali.

Sodium hydroxide is an alkali that is made when electricity passes through sodium chloride solution. It is used to turn wood chips into wood pulp for making paper like this.

Solution mining

Rock salt is often **extracted** from the ground by a process called solution mining. This avoids sending miners and all their equipment underground. A hole is drilled into the ground until it reaches the salt deposit, then three tubes are sunk in. Water is pumped down one tube into the salt, dissolving it and producing brine. Air is pumped down the second tube, which forces the brine to the surface through the third tube. The removal of too much salt from any one place is avoided to prevent the ground caving in. Even so, some of the underground caverns are huge. Their volume can be over a million cubic metres – easily enough to contain a cathedral or other large building!

Electrolysis cells

Hydrogen and chlorine can **react** together explosively, so they must be separated when electricity is passed through the brine. Three types of electrolysis cell are used to extract chlorine from brine. The oldest type is the mercury cell, which was developed at the end of the nineteenth century. Its positive electrodes are made from graphite and its negative electrode is a layer of mercury that flows along the bottom of the cell. When electricity is passed through the brine, chlorine is produced at the positive electrodes. It is piped off and stored ready for sale.

Extracting chlorine safely

In the mercury cell, sodium metal forms at the negative electrode, which dissolves into the mercury to form a mixture of two metals called an amalgam. When the amalgam flows out of the bottom of the cell, it is mixed with water. The sodium in the amalgam reacts with the water, producing hydrogen and sodium hydroxide. The mercury is then recycled.

The membrane cell, developed in the 1970s, has a positive electrode made from titanium and a negative electrode made from nickel. The hydrogen and chlorine are kept apart by a special layer, called the membrane. The membrane cell uses less electricity than the mercury cell and is environmentally friendly because no poisonous mercury is used.

Safe to drink

At water treatment plants chlorine **compounds** are added to our drinking water to kill harmful bacteria. You can sometimes smell the chlorine when you fill a glass of water from the tap.

Tackling typhoid

Typhoid is a disease caused by the bacterium *Salmonella typhi* that infects us when we swallow contaminated food or drink. Infected people suffer from fever and internal bleeding. Unless they are given antibiotics to kill the bacteria about a quarter of patients die. The UK and the USA started sterilizing public water supplies using chlorine compounds at the start of the last century. This reduced the number of deaths from typhoid dramatically.

This is a Salmonella *bacterium, magnified 10,000 times using an electron microscope. Typhoid is caused by* Salmonella, *so public water supplies are treated with chlorine compounds to kill harmful bacteria like these.*

Chlorine in the water

Before water is piped into our homes various chemicals are added to remove substances that make it coloured and cloudy; then it is filtered. Harmful bacteria in the water are killed by chlorination. This often involves adding chlorine gas itself to the water, although chlorine compounds may be used instead. These include sodium hypochlorite (NaOCl), which is a greenish-yellow liquid, sometimes called liquid bleach, or a white powder called calcium hypochlorite, $Ca(OCl)_2$. Just enough of these substances are added to kill bacteria, but not sufficient to harm us.

Don't mix chlorine and fish

Chlorinated water does not hurt us, but it kills aquarium fish. People who keep fish let the water stand for a day or so to let the chlorine escape into the air before adding it to their fish tanks. If they are in a hurry, they can add tablets containing sodium thiosulphate ($Na_2S_2O_3$), which **reacts** immediately with the chlorine to form harmless sodium chloride or salt.

Swimming with chlorine

Water in most swimming pools is chlorinated to kill harmful bacteria and to stop unsightly green algae growing in it. Chlorine gas can be used, but pool staff must be careful, as it is poisonous. It cannot be stored in basements in case it escapes and causes someone to be suffocated (chlorine is **denser** than air and would remain in the basement). Modern pools use sodium hypochlorite or more complex compounds such as Dichlor (sodium dichloroisocyanurate, $C_3Cl_2N_3NaO_3$).

Stinging eyes

If you get stinging eyes after swimming the water might have been too acidic or too alkaline, but it is more likely that chloramines were the culprits. These compounds cause strong 'chlorine' smells and form when chlorine in the water reacts with nitrogen compounds in sweat and urine. Swimmers should always have a shower before they enter the water to remove any sweat. Going to the toilet first is a good idea too!

Bleaches and bangs

Sodium chlorate ($NaCl_3O$) is a herbicide, which means that it kills plants. It is absorbed through leaves and roots, killing all green plants, not just weeds. Herbicides that contain sodium chlorate are not normally used to control weeds in crops, but they are widely used to control plants that grow on railway lines and by the roadside. Other chlorine **compounds** are used as bleaches and **oxidizing agents** in rocket fuels.

Back to white

Household bleaches are liquids used to clean and disinfect many areas of our homes. Their active ingredient, sodium hypochlorite, kills harmful bacteria, so they are used to clean and disinfect kitchen worktops, sinks, floors and toilets. Bleaching powder, which contains calcium hypochlorite, is used in a similar way. Some people use bleach, diluted with water, to remove difficult stains from their laundry. However, it is best to only bleach items that are already white, such as nappies and sheets, as the bleach also removes the colour.

Paper is made from wood pulp. Chips of wood are boiled with sodium hydroxide and sodium sulphite. This produces dark brown paper, only suitable for grocery bags and cardboard. To make white paper and card, the brown colour must be removed from the wood pulp using bleach. This is usually calcium hypochlorite, sodium hypochlorite or sodium chlorite ($NaClO_2$).

A simple laboratory test for chlorine

There is a simple laboratory test to see if chlorine gas is produced in a chemical **reaction**. Damp blue litmus paper is held over the mouth of the test tube, containing the reacting chemicals. If chlorine gas is being produced, the litmus paper turns red and then white shortly afterwards. This happens because an acid is produced when the chlorine dissolves in the damp litmus paper, turning it red, but eventually the chlorine bleaches the litmus paper white.

Fireworks and fuel

The Chinese discovered gunpowder over a thousand years ago. They found that a mixture of carbon, sulphur and potassium nitrate would burn violently if they ignited it. The potassium nitrate (KNO_3) is the oxidizing agent in the mixture, which means that it provides the oxygen needed for the gunpowder to burn. The oxidizing agent in modern fireworks is usually potassium chlorate ($KClO_3$). Rockets that launch satellites into space use solid fuels that contain ammonium perchlorate (NH_4ClO_4) as the oxidizing agent. The solid rocket boosters for the Space Shuttle are the largest ever made. Each of them contains 500 tonnes of fuel, which includes 350 tonnes of ammonium perchlorate.

▲
Modern fireworks like these, exploding over the Sydney Harbour Bridge in Australia, contain potassium chlorate to help the gunpowder burn faster.

Plastics and solvents

Chlordane ($C_{10}H_6Cl_8$), a thick, amber-coloured liquid with a faint smell of chlorine, is an insecticide and has been used to control termites and other insects. Many countries have banned chlordane because it is a 'persistent organic pollutant'. These are poisonous substances that build up in the environment and damage living things, including us. There are many other complex **molecules** containing chlorine that are still very useful, however.

Plastic fantastic

Polyvinyl chloride (PVC) is a plastic that contains chlorine. PVC accounts for a quarter of all the world's plastic and around thirty million tonnes of it are produced in the world each year. PVC is difficult to use on its own, so chemicals are added to produce different types of PVC. Soft PVC is used to make items such as raincoats, garden hoses and soles for shoes. Blood donor bags and insulation for electrical wires are made from flexible PVC, while more rigid PVC is useful for making bottles and food containers. Very tough PVC is used to make water pipes, window frames and panels for buildings. Unfortunately, although PVC resists burning, once it is on fire it releases poisonous fumes, and it is not **biodegradeable**.

From monomers to polymers

PVC and other **polymers** are made by joining together lots of smaller molecules, called **monomers**. The monomer for PVC is vinyl chloride or chloroethene (C_2H_3Cl). Vinyl chloride molecules can join together, end to end in a long chain, to make polyvinyl chloride.

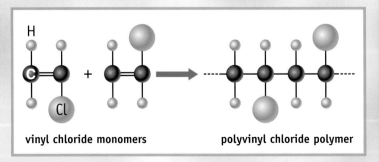

vinyl chloride monomers   polyvinyl chloride polymer

Time to sleep

General anaesthetics are chemicals that cause you to fall asleep, ready for a surgical operation. Chloroform (trichloromethane, $CHCl_3$) is a colourless liquid that can be used as an anaesthetic for operations. It was first used as a general anaesthetic in 1847, but it was difficult to get the dose right and someone died from chloroform poisoning only a year later, so other anaesthetics such as halothane ($CF_3CHClBr$) were developed to make operations safer. Chloroform is a good **solvent**, dissolving substances that are insoluble in water such as oil and grease. There are many other solvents that contain chlorine, like dichloromethane (CH_2Cl_2) and tetrachloromethane (CCl_4). In the past, these substances were widely used in scientific research, industrial processes and for dry-cleaning clothes. Unfortunately, just like CFCs, these **compounds** can damage the Earth's ozone layer and are being banned.

◀ *Chloroform was first used as a general anaesthetic in 1847. Early equipment was primitive and it was difficult to get the dose right.*

Chlorofluorocarbons

Chlorofluorocarbons (CFCs) are compounds that contain chlorine, fluorine, carbon and hydrogen **atoms**. They did have many everyday uses, for instance as propellants in aerosol spray cans, blowing agents to make insulating bubbles of gas in fast-food containers, dry-cleaning fluids and cooling liquids in refrigerators. Most of them have been banned because they damage the ozone layer.

◀ *This diagram (opposite) shows how short molecules of vinyl chloride join together to form a long molecule of polyvinyl chloride (PVC). There may be thousands of these monomer molecules in one long polymer molecule.*

CFCs and the ozone layer

Nearly all CFCs are banned now or will be soon, as they are damaging the Earth's ozone layer. To understand why this is so worrying, it helps to know a bit about the chemistry of the atmosphere.

Ozone

Ordinary oxygen **molecules**, the sort we breathe in to stay alive, are each made from two oxygen **atoms** joined together by chemical **bonds**. Ozone molecules contain three oxygen atoms joined together in a ring. Ozone is poisonous and causes stinging eyes and breathing difficulties, so why are we so concerned about the ozone layer in the atmosphere disappearing?

The ozone layer

Nearly all the ozone in the atmosphere is concentrated in the stratosphere, which is between 10 km (6 miles) and 50 km (30 miles) above the Earth's surface. It is not a layer as such, but is thinly mixed with other gases. Although the Sun provides the heat and light that living things need, it also bombards the Earth with harmful ultraviolet light that can damage crops and cause skin cancer. The ozone layer is very important because it absorbs ultraviolet light, protecting us from it.

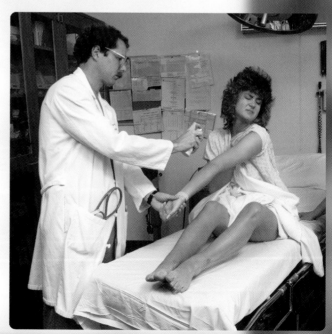

Exposure to too much ultraviolet light from the Sun causes sunburn like this and can lead to skin cancer. Ozone in the upper atmosphere blocks a lot of this harmful ultraviolet light, but it is being destroyed by CFCs.

Holes and Poles

Ozone molecules in the ozone layer naturally break down to form ordinary oxygen molecules, which then **react** together to make ozone again. However, if ozone molecules break down faster than new ones are made, the amount of ozone in the stratosphere goes down and we get a 'hole' in the ozone layer. The biggest holes appear over the North and South Poles because of the way the atmosphere moves there, but holes have also appeared over northern Europe and other areas.

CFCs in the atmosphere

CFCs or chlorofluorocarbons, are usually unreactive chemicals that cause few problems at ground level. However, once they are released into the atmosphere and reach the stratosphere, ultraviolet light from the Sun breaks them down, releasing very reactive chlorine and fluorine atoms. These atoms break down ozone faster than it can be remade, causing the concentration of ozone to fall. This produces a 'hole' in the ozone layer, which allows more harmful ultraviolet light to reach the Earth's surface.

The Montreal Protocol

The Montreal Protocol is an international agreement, signed in Canada in 1987, that controls the manufacture and use of substances that damage the ozone layer, including CFCs. The manufacture of most of them has been banned in nearly all countries and many of them have been replaced by hydrochlorofluorocarbons (HCFCs). Although HCFCs cause less damage to the ozone layer, they will no longer be made either by 2040. The ozone layer should then recover by the middle of this century.

▲

*Many older refrigerators contain chlorofluorocarbons (CFCs). These are **compounds** that contain chlorine and fluorine. CFCs were used in the insulating foam and cooling liquid, but most of them are banned now.*

Bromine

Bromine is red-brown and the only non-metal **element** that is liquid at room temperature. It is **denser** than water: a litre of bromine would weigh 3.1 kg, whereas a litre of water weighs just 1 kg. Bromine easily vaporizes, producing a red vapour with an unpleasant, sharp smell, similar to the smell of chlorine. Bromine liquid and vapour are poisonous and cause dangerous burns if they come into contact with skin. This makes bromine difficult and dangerous to handle.

From stench to bromine

Bromine was discovered in 1826 by a French chemist, Antoine Balard, who was only 23 years old. Balard **extracted** various chemicals from seawater and seaweed ashes and added chlorine water to produce iodine. An orange-yellow layer sometimes formed when he did this, which Balard removed and distilled, producing liquid bromine. At first he thought that the liquid was a chlorine **compound**, but as he could not break it down into anything else, Balard decided that he had discovered a new element. He named bromine after the Greek word meaning stench, as it has an unpleasant smell.

Don't take too long to write up your experiments

Balard was not the first person to discover bromine. Several other chemists found it at about the same time, but thought that it was a chlorine compound. Carl Löwig, a chemistry student at the University of Heidelberg in Germany, made some bromine at home a year before Balard. Unfortunately, he took too long to finish his experiments and publish his results, so Balard got the credit for bromine's discovery.

The water in the Dead Sea contains about ten times more salt than ordinary seawater. This means it is denser than seawater, so bathers easily float in it. The Dead Sea is also a rich source of bromine compounds.

Brine and bromine

Bromine is too **reactive** to be found naturally as a pure element, but **minerals** such as bromargyrite (silver bromide, AgBr) contain bromine compounds. Seawater has low concentrations of sodium bromide and other bromine compounds. Some salt waters naturally contain high concentrations of bromide, including the Dead Sea. Each litre of the water from this salt lake between Jordan and Israel contains about five grams of bromide. Around half a million tonnes of bromine are extracted each year, mainly in the USA, Israel, China and the UK.

Pushing out bromine

Bromine is extracted from seawater or other brines by bubbling chlorine gas through it. Chlorine is more reactive than bromine, so chlorine **displaces** it from its compounds. The displaced bromine dissolves in the water. Before the bromine is extracted and purified there are several more steps.

The word equation for extracting bromine using chlorine is:

sodium bromide + chlorine ⟶ bromine + sodium chloride

Uses of bromine compounds

Nearly a quarter of the bromine produced is used to make chemicals for the oil industry. When an oil well is drilled into the ground to reach oil, drilling fluids are needed to lubricate the drill bit as it works and later on to help keep the oil and gas flowing. Salts containing bromine are **dense** and drilling fluids often contain sodium bromide, calcium bromide or zinc bromide to increase their density, helping them work their way down the oil well.

▲ *Bromine compounds are widely used by the oil industry. They are used in drilling fluids that lubricate drill bits when they cut through rock, deep under the Earth's surface.*

Dyeing to be Roman

Wealthy Romans wore togas dyed with a purple bromine **compound**. The Romans did not know that the dye contained bromine, but they did know where to get it. The dye was **extracted** from the glands of a sea snail called *Murex* in a complex process lasting several days. Over nine thousand snails were needed to produce one gram of dye, which made it very expensive and only the wealthiest Romans could afford it. The dye industry was based around Tyre, an important trading port on the Mediterranean coast in Roman times, so the dye was called Tyrian purple or royal purple. Dibromoindigo is the chemical that produces the colour in the dye and it was first made artificially in 1903.

Fire – keep back!

The biggest single use of bromine is in the manufacture of fire retardants; nearly half the bromine produced is used in this way. Plastics are used almost everywhere, in cars, homes and factories. Once they are alight, they burn fiercely to produce a lot of heat and thick, poisonous smoke. Fire retardants are chemicals that make it more difficult for these materials to catch fire and for the flames to spread. If flames touch the treated plastic, the fire retardant breaks down, using up some of the heat. A layer of hydrogen bromide is produced that insulates the plastic and keeps oxygen away from it. The bromine in the fire retardant also interferes with the chemical **reactions** needed for the plastic to burn.

Not too strong or too weak – just right

*The other halogens are not as good as bromine for making fire retardants because they form chemical **bonds** that are either too strong or too weak. Fluorine-carbon bonds are too strong, so fluorine cannot interfere with the fire very well. Iodine-carbon bonds are too weak, so iodine is lost too easily. Chlorine-carbon bonds and bromine-carbon bonds are just right. However, if the fire retardant contains bromine instead of chlorine, less is needed.*

Bromine and health

In the nineteenth century, potassium bromide was used as a medicine to control epilepsy, an illness that causes people and animals to have seizures or fits. People are now given other medicines, but veterinary surgeons may still prescribe potassium bromide or sodium bromide to control epilepsy in dogs. However, bromine is still an important ingredient in the manufacture of modern medicines used for people.

Coughs and sneezes spread diseases

Bromine **compounds** are often used during the manufacture of some medicines, such as painkillers, even though the final product does not contain bromine. Many medicines however do contain bromine compounds, such as dextromethorphan hydrobromide, which is used in cough medicine. This does not relieve the pain of a sore throat, but it helps us to cough less when it is tickly by putting a lining on the throat. Another bromine compound, bromopheniramine maleate, is used as an antihistamine. People with hay fever (an allergy to pollen) can suffer terribly from runny noses and itchy eyes. Antihistamines help to reduce the symptoms of hay fever and other allergies.

People who are allergic to pollen suffer from hay fever, which causes runny noses and itchy eyes. Some bromine compounds are antihistamines. These are medicines that relieve the symptoms of allergies like hay fever. ▶

Halothane

An anaesthetic containing bromine, called halothane, has been used since the middle of the last century. Each molecule of halothane ($CF_3CHClBr$) contains three out of the five halogens, namely fluorine, chlorine and bromine. Halothane is a liquid at room temperature, but easily turns into a vapour so the patient can breathe it in.

Pest control

Huge amounts of water are used in many industrial processes, such as paper-making and brewing. Meanwhile, power stations and large commercial air-conditioning systems use water for cooling. It is important that dangerous bacteria, fungi and algae do not grow in the water or the equipment, so 'biocides' are added to the water. Biocides are chemicals that kill unwanted organisms. Sodium bromide or bromine chloride is often used.

▲
Cooling towers like these are needed by power stations as part of their normal operation. A draught of air cools the hot water as it falls inside the tower. Bromine compounds may be used to kill algae and other unwanted organisms that could grow there.

Methyl bromide (CH_3Br) is a poisonous and colourless gas. It is very good at killing all sorts of pests that reduce crops, such as mice, certain insects, harmful fungi and some microscopic worms called nematodes. Methyl bromide is applied to the soil to sterilize it before crops are planted and to protect stored food from pests. Unfortunately, it is also very good at destroying the ozone layer. Many countries have agreed to stop using it by 2005 under the Montreal Protocol.

Iodine

Like the other halogens, iodine **molecules** are made from two **atoms** joined together, but iodine is solid at room temperature, unlike fluorine and chlorine, which are gases, and bromine, which is a liquid. This is because iodine has stronger forces between its molecules. Iodine crystals are shiny and so dark that they look almost black, but they easily turn into a purple vapour. Iodine has a sharp, unpleasant smell and is poisonous. It dissolves slightly in water to produce a brown solution.

From burnt seaweed to iodine

Iodine was discovered in 1811 by Bernard Courtois, a French chemical manufacturer. Various chemicals were produced in his factory from seaweed. The seaweed was collected and burnt, then the ashes were treated to **extract** the **compounds** they contained. Courtois discovered iodine by accident when he added too much concentrated sulphuric acid one day.

A purple vapour appeared, which formed black crystals when it touched cold surfaces. Iodine was named after the Greek word for violet coloured.

▶ This is bladder wrack, a type of seaweed that is a rich source of iodine compounds. The air-filled bladders allow the fronds to float.

The word equation for the reaction between sodium iodide and concentrated sulphuric acid is:

sodium iodine + suphuric acid → iodine + sodium hydrogensulphate + water + sulphur dioxide

Subliming on a cold finger

Iodine is an unusual substance because it does not form a liquid. If solid iodine is heated it turns directly into a vapour and when the vapour is cooled the opposite happens. This is called subliming. Chemists use a 'cold finger' to sublime iodine vapour, but not their own! Instead they use a glass test tube containing cold water. When the iodine vapour touches the cold glass, it sublimes to form solid crystals on the surface.

◀ *Iodine forms dark, shiny crystals that easily turn into a purple vapour when heated.*

Extracting iodine

Iodine is not found naturally as a free **element** because, like the other halogens, it is too **reactive**. Iodine compounds such as iodargyrite (silver iodide) are rare, but there is some sodium iodate in a **mineral** called Chile saltpetre (sodium nitrate), which is abundant. Iodine compounds are present in very low concentrations in seawater. However, brown seaweed such as bladder wrack concentrates iodine compounds in its cells, which is why Courtois was able to find iodine in seaweed ash.

Nearly twenty thousand tonnes of iodine are produced each year worldwide. Chile and Japan produce 85 per cent and the rest comes mostly from the USA. Commercial extraction of iodine is mainly from brines, but in Japan it is obtained from seaweed. Different methods are used to extract iodine, depending on whether it is found as an iodide or iodate. In each case, several steps are needed to produce pure iodine.

Iodine and food

Iodine crystals dissolve slightly in water, killing most of the bacteria in it. This makes the water safe to drink, although rather brown and smelly.

Fit to drink

Iodine water purification tablets contain a complex mixture of glycine, hydriodic acid and iodine. They dissolve in water, killing most bacteria within twenty minutes. The smell and taste of the iodine can be removed by adding ascorbic acid tablets. Iodine water purification is useful for hikers and campers, but it is also very important if the mains supply becomes contaminated, for example after floods.

Starch testing

Foods such as rice, bread and pasta contain a lot of starch. This is a carbohydrate needed in our diet to give us energy. Biologists can find out if a food contains starch by testing it with iodine solution. This is a mixture of iodine and potassium iodide, dissolved in water. When iodine solution is added to food, it turns purple if it contains starch.

A purple colour forms when iodine solution is added to a test tube of starch suspension. As a result, iodine is used to test plant leaves and foods, such as bread and rice, to see if they contain starch.

Photosynthesis and starch

Plants make their own food by a process called photosynthesis. Carbon dioxide and water **react** together in the plant cells, using energy from light, to make sugars such as glucose. The glucose is converted into starch, which is stored in the plant cells until the plant needs it. Biologists find out if plants have been photosynthesizing by testing the leaves for starch with iodine solution. The leaf turns purple wherever it contains starch.

An oily number

Fat is an important part of our diet, but if we eat too much saturated fat we have an increased risk of developing heart disease. Food scientists use iodine monochloride (ICl) to find out how saturated a particular fat is.

Fats and oils contain long chains of carbon **atoms** joined together by chemical **bonds**. Saturated fats, like butter and lard, tend to be hard at room temperature and their carbon atoms are all joined to each other by single chemical bonds. When some of the carbon atoms are joined by double bonds (two bonds at once), this makes the fat unsaturated and softer. If a lot of carbon atoms are joined by double bonds, the fat is polyunsaturated and liquid at room temperature. Most vegetable oils and fish oils are polyunsaturated.

Iodine monochloride reacts with the double bonds in the fats – the more unsaturated the fat, the more iodine monochloride reacts. The scientists convert the results into a number called the 'iodine number'. Butter has an iodine number of about 35 and is quite solid at room temperature, while runny peanut oil has an iodine number of about 90.

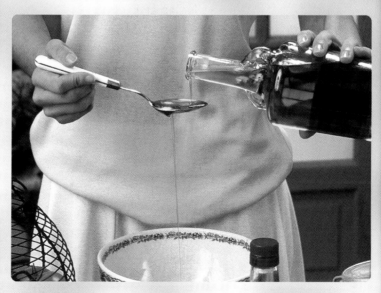

▲
Iodine monochloride is used by food scientists to see how unsaturated a fat or oil might be. Runny vegetable oils like this are very unsaturated and have a high iodine number.

Iodine and health

Iodine is an important trace **mineral** in our diet. It is a vital component of two hormones produced by the thyroid, a gland in the front of the neck, just below the voice box. If we do not get enough iodine, we can suffer from various disorders.

Iodine deficiency disorders

If the thyroid gland cannot make the two thyroid hormones we suffer from 'hypothyroidism'. Adults with hypothyroidism feel run down, tired, cold and may suffer from muscle pains. The thyroid hormones are needed for proper growth and development in children, so iodine deficiency can be very serious for them.

Goitre and Derbyshire Neck

Goitre, pronounced 'goy-ter', is an obvious symptom of iodine deficiency. It is a bulge in the neck caused by the thyroid gland getting bigger as it tries to keep making hormones, even though there is not enough iodine. Goitre was very common in the county of Derbyshire, UK and used to be known as 'Derbyshire Neck'. This is because the limestone in Derbyshire indirectly prevents iodine entering the human food chain.

This woman has goitre, a swelling in the neck caused by the thyroid gland getting bigger. This often happens if there is too little iodine in the diet.

Pregnant women with iodine deficiency can give birth to babies that weigh less than normal. The babies may also suffer from brain damage, which causes learning difficulties. In severe cases, the children may make very slow progress, be very short and have difficulty controlling their muscles properly. These problems cannot be reversed, even if the children later get enough iodine in their diet. About fifty million children suffer from iodine deficiency disorders and over a billion people in the world are at risk from them, yet they are easily preventable.

Iodized salt

Many countries add iodine **compounds** to table salt, especially where crops are grown in soil containing little iodine. Iodized salt is very successful at preventing iodine deficiency disorders. It usually contains potassium iodate, which is more stable than iodide when salt is stored. All the table salt sold in Canada and about half of the salt sold in the USA is iodized. All cattle food sold in the UK must be iodized by law. This means that milk and milk products contain iodine, so salt is not usually iodized in the UK, although it is available.

Ouch! – treating wounds

'Tincture of iodine' is used as an antiseptic to treat wounds. It contains ethanol (alcohol) and a solution of potassium iodide and iodine. However, it stains skin and clothing and can only be used to clean around the wound as it damages the cut skin. Tincture of iodine has been largely replaced by a substance called povidone-iodine because of these drawbacks. Surgeons use it to disinfect their hands and to prepare their patients' skin before operations. It is also widely used to treat wounds and burns.

◀ *Surgeons 'scrub up' before operations, using cleaning solutions, containing iodine compounds that produce the orange colour seen here.*

Radioactive iodine

Naturally occurring iodine is made from an **isotope** called iodine-127, but other isotopes are made artificially in nuclear reactors and nuclear explosions. Iodine-127 is not **radioactive**, but its artificial isotopes are. This makes them useful for some types of medical scans and scientific research, but they can be dangerous.

Follow that protein

Biochemists study the chemistry of living things. They often need to investigate proteins from cells, but because the amounts are very tiny this is difficult to do. Biochemists use chemicals called 'tracers' to follow the proteins in their experiments. Iodine-125 is often used as a tracer because it produces gamma **radiation**, which is like X-rays, but more powerful. We cannot feel or see gamma radiation, but it is easily detected using radiation detectors such as a Geiger counter. The biochemists use chemical **reactions** to attach minute amounts of iodine-125 to the proteins. This is called radiolabelling and allows them to trace a protein's movements by detecting the radiation it gives off.

The Chernobyl Disaster

In April 1986, there was a terrible accident at a nuclear power station near Chernobyl, a town 100 km (60 miles) north of Kiev in the Ukraine. An experiment carried out during the night went wrong, causing a steam explosion that blew the lid off the reactor. The reactor caught fire after another explosion and burned for ten days. Half of the radioactive iodine-131 it contained was released and carried by the wind all over Europe – some of it even reached parts of the USA. This was very serious because it contaminated farmland, rainwater and food.

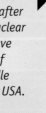

This computer simulation shows the spread of radioactivity ten days after the accident at the Chernobyl nuclear power station in 1986. Winds have carried radioactivity thousands of kilometres over Europe, the Middle East, Asia and even parts of the USA.

Just like ordinary iodine, radioactive iodine-131 concentrates in the thyroid gland once it gets into the body through food and drink. If the thyroid gland is exposed to too much radiation, it may become cancerous. To reduce the chance of this happening, people living close to the reactor were given tablets containing non-radioactive iodine, which diluted the radioactive iodine in their bodies. Even so, many people in the area developed thyroid cancer later.

Checking the thyroid gland

If our thyroid gland stops working properly, doctors can investigate the problem by doing a scan involving iodine-131. A small amount of the radioactive substance is injected into the patient's bloodstream that concentrates in the thyroid gland. A camera is held near the patient's neck, which detects the small amount of gamma radiation emitted and a picture of the thyroid gland is made. The procedure is safe because only very tiny amounts of iodine-131 are used.

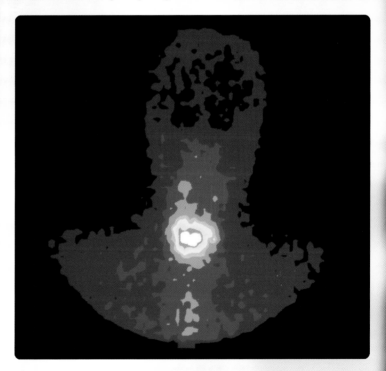

▲
This is a medical scan showing the thyroid gland in a patient's neck. The patient was injected with radioactive iodine-131. This concentrated in the thyroid where it was detected using a special camera sensitive to gamma radiation.

Astatine

Astatine is extremely rare, so it is very difficult to investigate its chemical and physical properties. Most of the information about astatine has been estimated by studying the other **elements** in **group** 7 and following the trends in their properties (see chapter 5). It is the least **reactive** of the halogens and probably a shiny black solid at room temperature. Chemists cannot study the reactions of astatine in test tubes because there is not enough of it at any one time, so they use complex machines to detect what happens when a few astatine **atoms** react with other elements. From these experiments, chemists believe that astatine is a metalloid, which means that it has some properties of metals and some of non-metals. Astatine is closest to iodine in its chemical reactions.

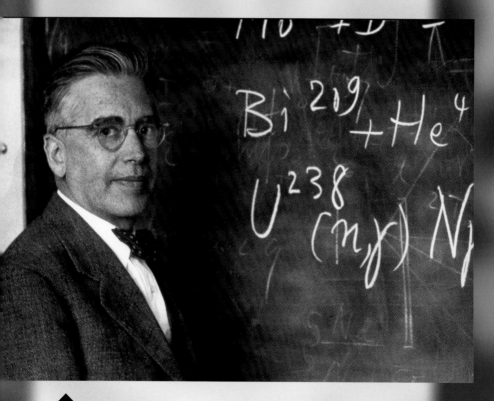

▲
The Italian physicist Emilio Segré was one of the scientists who first made astatine in 1940. He is seen here 12 years later next to a chalk board that shows part of the equation for the nuclear reaction that forms astatine.

The discovery of astatine

A gap was left in the **periodic table** where an element was thought to exist, but was still undiscovered. Chemists were keen to find the missing element and fill the gap, but it quickly became clear that they would have to make it. As elements cannot be changed into other elements by chemical reactions, **nuclear reactions** were needed to do this.

Nuclear reactions can change the **nucleus** of an element into that of another element. Dale Corson, Kenneth MacKenzie and Emilio Segré made some astatine in 1940, while working at the Lawrence Berkeley National Laboratory in California. They used a machine called a cyclotron to join helium nuclei and bismuth nuclei together to make astatine.

The nuclear reaction for producing astatine is:

$$\underset{\text{helium}}{^{4}_{2}\text{He}} + \underset{\text{bismuth}}{^{209}_{83}\text{Bi}} \rightarrow \underset{\text{astatine}}{^{211}_{85}\text{At}} + \underset{\text{neutron radiation}}{2^{1}_{0}\text{n}}$$

*The equation shows a helium nucleus joining on to a bismuth nucleus. This makes an astatine nucleus and two **neutrons** that shoot away at high speed as neutron **radiation**.*

Even rarer than you think

Astatine is still made using nuclear reactions and only millionths of a gram are available to study. Worse still, astatine is **radioactive** and breaks down very quickly to form bismuth again. Its longest lasting **isotope**, astatine-210, has a **half-life** of just eight hours. This means that every eight hours, half of the remaining astatine breaks down into bismuth. In fact, the name astatine comes from Greek words meaning 'not lasting'! Astatine is formed naturally from the nuclear decay or break down of uranium-235, but it is estimated that there is less than a gram of astatine in the Earth's crust at any time. Astatine has no practical uses.

Find out more about the halogens

The table below contains some information about the properties of the halogens.

Element	Symbol	Atomic number	Melting point (°C)	Boiling point (°C)	State at 25°C	Density at 25°C (g/cm³)
fluorine	F	9	−220	−188	gas	0.00078
chlorine	Cl	17	−101	−34	gas	0.00145
bromine	Br	35	−7	59	liquid	3.12
iodine	I	53	114	184	solid	4.93
astatine	At	85	302	337	solid	not known

Compounds

These tables show you the chemical formulae of most of the **compounds** mentioned in this book. For example, sodium sulphate has the formula Na_2SO_4. This means it is made from two sodium **atoms**, one sulphur atom and four oxygen atoms, joined together by chemical **bonds**.

Fluorine compounds

Fluorine compounds	Formula
cryolite	Na_3AlF_6
fluorspar (calcium fluoride)	CaF_2
gold fluoride	AuF_3
halothane	$CF_3CHClBr$
hexafluorosilicic acid	H_2SiF_6
hydrogen fluoride	HF
silver fluoride	AgF
sodium fluoride	NaF
sodium hexafluorosilicate	Na_2SiF_6
sodium monofluorophosphate	Na_2PO_3F
sulphur hexafluoride	SF_6
tetrafluoroethene	C_2F_4
xenon difluoride	XeF_2

Chlorine compounds	Formula
halite	NaCl
sylvite	KCl
carnallite	$KMgCl_3$
ammonium perchlorate	NH_4ClO_4
calcium hypochlorite	$Ca(OCl)_2$
chlordane	$C_{10}H_6Cl_8$
halothane	$CF_3CHClBr$
hydrogen chloride	HCl
iodine monochloride	ICl
iron chloride	$FeCl_3$
potassium chloride	KCl
potassium chlorate	$KClO_3$
silver chloride	AgCl
sodium chloride	NaCl
sodium hypochlorite	NaOCl
sodium chlorite	$NaOCl_2$
sodium chlorate	$NaClO_3$
sodium dichloroisocyanurate	$C_3Cl_2N_3NaO_3$
dichloromethane	CH_2Cl_2
trichloromethane (chloroform)	$CHCl_3$
tetrachloromethane	CCl_4
vinyl chloride (chloroethene)	C_2H_3Cl

Bromine compounds	Formula
bromargyrite	AgBr
bromopheniramine maleate	$C_{16}H_{19}BrN_2.C_4H_4O_4$
dextromethorphan hydrobromide	$C_{18}H_{25}NO.HBr.H_2O$
dibromoindigo	$C_{16}H_8Br_2N_2O_2$
halothane	$CF_3CHClBr$
hydrogen bromide	HBr
iron bromide	$FeBr_3$
methyl bromide	CH_3Br
potassium bromide	KBr
silver bromide	AgBr
sodium bromide	NaBr

Find out more continued

Iodine compounds

Iodine compounds	Formula
hydrogen iodide	HI
iodargyrite	AgI
iodine monochloride	ICl
iron iodide	FeI_3
potassium iodate	KIO_3
potassium iodide	KI
silver iodide	AgI
sodium iodate	$NaIO_3$
sodium iodide	NaI

Acids

Acids	Formula
hexafluorosilicic acid	H_2SiF_6
hydrofluoric acid	HF
hydrochloric acid	HCl
hydrobromic acid	HBr
hydriodic acid	HI
hypochlorous acid	HOCl
hypobromous acid	HOBr
hypoiodous acid	HOI
nitric acid	HNO_3
sulphuric acid	H_2SO_4

Other compounds

Other compounds	Formula
calcium sulphate	$CaSO_4$
potassium manganate(VII)	$KMnO_4$
potassium nitrate	KNO_3
silver nitrate	$AgNO_3$
sodium hydroxide	NaOH
sodium nitrate	$NaNO_3$
sodium sulphite	Na_2SO_3
sodium thiosulphate	$Na_2S_2O_3$
sulphur dioxide	SO_2
uranium oxide	UO_3
water	H_2O

Glossary

atom smallest particle of an element that has the properties of that element. Atoms contain smaller particles called subatomic particles.

atomic number number of protons in the nucleus of an atom. It is also called the proton number. No two elements have the same atomic number.

biodegradable material that can be broken down by bacteria or in the environment

bond force that joins atoms together

compound substance made from the atoms of two or more elements, joined together by chemical bonds. Compounds can be broken down into simpler substances and they have different properties from the elements in them. Water, for example, is a liquid at room temperature, but it is made from two gases, hydrogen and oxygen.

density mass of a substance compared to its volume. The density of a substance is its mass divided by its volume. Substances with a high density feel very heavy for their size.

displacement reaction reaction where a more reactive element pushes out or displaces a less reactive element from its compounds

electrolysis breaking down or decomposing a compound by passing electricity through it. The compound must be molten or dissolved in a liquid for electrolysis to work.

electron subatomic particle with a negative electric charge. Electrons are found around the nucleus of an atom.

element substance made from one type of atom. Elements cannot be broken down into simpler substances. All substances are made from one or more elements.

enzyme protein that is a catalyst, assisting in chemical reactions without itself being used up

extract remove a chemical from a mixture of chemicals

group vertical column of elements in the periodic table. Elements in a group have similar properties.

half-life time taken for half the atoms of a radioactive substance to decay

ion charged particle made when atoms lose or gain electrons. If a metal atom loses electrons it becomes a positive ion. If a non-metal atom gains electrons it becomes a negative ion.

isotope atom of an element with the same number of protons and electrons, but different numbers of neutrons. Different isotopes share the same atomic number, but they have a different mass number.

mass number number of protons added to the number of neutrons, in the nucleus of an atom

mineral substance that is found naturally, but does not come from animals or plants. Metal ores and limestone are examples of minerals.

molecule smallest particle of an element or compound that exists by itself. A molecule is usually made from two or more atoms joined together.

monomer small molecule that can join end to end to make larger molecules called polymers

neutralize neutral solution made when an acid and an alkali or a base react together. A neutral solution means it is not acidic or alkaline.

neutron subatomic particle with no electric charge. Neutrons are found in the nucleus of an atom.

nuclear reaction reaction involving the nucleus of an atom. Radiation is produced in nuclear reactions.

nucleus part of an atom made from protons and neutrons. It has a positive electric charge and is found at the centre of the atom.

oxidizing agent chemical that can add oxygen to an element or compound in a chemical reaction. These are also called oxidants.

period horizontal row of elements in the periodic table

periodic table table in which all the known elements are arranged into groups and periods

polymer large molecule made by joining smaller molecules called monomers together. Plastics are polymers.

precipitate solid that forms in a liquid during a chemical reaction

proton subatomic particle with a positive electric charge. Protons are found in the nucleus of an atom.

proton number number of protons in the nucleus of an atom. It is also called the atomic number. No two elements have the same proton number.

radiation energy or particles given off in a nuclear reaction

radioactive substance that can produce radiation

reaction chemical change that produces new substances

solvent substance, usually a liquid, that can dissolve other substances

subatomic particle particle smaller than an atom, such as a proton, a neutron or an electron

Timeline

chlorine discovered	1774	Carl Scheele
iodine discovered	1811	Bernard Courtois
bromine discovered	1826	Antoine-Jérôme Balard
'Talbotype' patented	1841	William Fox Talbot
fluorine discovered	1886	Henri Moissan
poly(tetrafluoroethene) or ETFE discovered	1938	Roy Plunkett
astatine discovered	1940	Dale Corson, Kenneth MacKenzie and Emilio Segré
agreement signed, controlling substances damaging to the ozone layer, such as CFC's	1987	Montreal protocol

Further reading and useful websites

Books

Knapp, Brian, *The Elements* series, particularly, *Chlorine, Fluorine, Bromine and Iodine* (Atlantic Europe Publishing Co., 1996)

Oxlade, Chris, *Chemicals in Action* series, particularly, *Atoms* (Heinemann Library, 2002)

Oxlade, Chris, *Chemicals in Action* series, particularly, *Elements and Compounds* (Heinemann Library, 2002)

Websites

WebElements™
http://www.webelements.com
An interactive periodic table crammed with information and photographs.

Proton Don
http://www.funbrain.com/periodic
The fun periodic table quiz!

Mineralogy Database
http://www.webmineral.com
Useful information about minerals, including colour photographs and their chemistry.

DiscoverySchool
http://school.discovery.com/clipart
Help for science projects and homework, and free science clip art.

BBC Science
http://www.bbc.co.uk/science
Quizzes, news, information and games about all areas of science.

Creative Chemistry http://www.creative-chemistry.org.uk
An interactive chemistry site with fun practical activities, quizzes, puzzles and more.

Index

Titles in the *Periodic Table* series include:

Hardback   0 431 16995 0

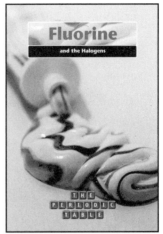

Hardback   0 431 16997 7

Hardback   0 431 16998 5

Hardback   0 431 16996 9

Hardback   0 431 16994 2

Hardback   0 431 16999 3

Find out about the other titles in this series on our website www.heinemann.co.uk/library